C000218650

Nelson English

Workbook 2

This book belongs to

_____

Sarah Lindsay and Wendy Wren

OXFORD
UNIVERSITY PRESS

OXFORD
UNIVERSITY PRESS

Great Clarendon Street, Oxford, OX2 6DP, United Kingdom

Oxford University Press is a department of the University of Oxford.
It furthers the University's objective of excellence in research, scholarship,
and education by publishing worldwide. Oxford is a registered trade mark
of Oxford University Press in the UK and in certain other countries.

Text © Sarah Lindsay and Wendy Wren 2018
The moral rights of the author have been asserted.

First published 2018

All rights reserved. No part of this publication may be reproduced, stored in a retrieval
system, or transmitted, in any form or by any means, without the prior permission
in writing of Oxford University Press, or as expressly permitted by law, by licence or
under terms agreed with the appropriate reprographics rights organization. Enquiries
concerning reproduction outside the scope of the above should be sent to the Rights
Department, Oxford University Press, at the address above.

You must not circulate this work in any other form and you must impose this same
condition on any acquirer.

British Library Cataloguing in Publication Data

Data available

ISBN: 978-0-1984-1989-1

7 9 10 8 6

Paper used in the production of this book is a natural, recyclable product made from
wood grown in sustainable forests. The manufacturing process conforms to the
environmental regulations of the country of origin.

Printed in China by Colden Cup

Acknowledgements
Series consultant: John Jackman

Cover and inside illustrations by Q2A Media Services Inc.

Page make-up by Aptara

The publisher and authors would like to thank the following for permission to use photographs and
other copyright material:

p11(b): Shutterstock.

Contents

Vocabulary

Compound words

A Draw a line to join the pictures that make a **compound word**.

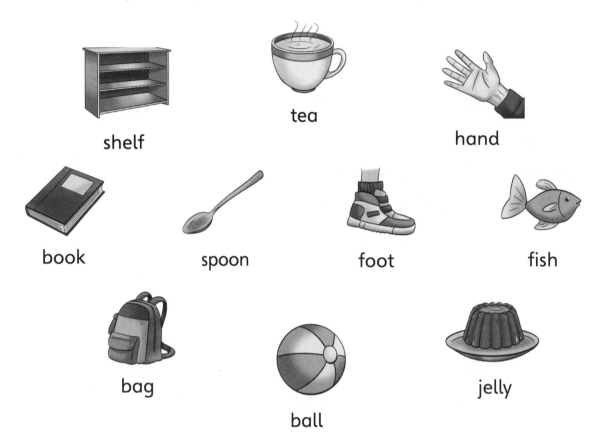

shelf

tea

hand

book

spoon

foot

fish

bag

ball

jelly

B Write the compound words you have made.

_____   _____   _____

_____   _____

Punctuation

Capital letters and full stops

A **sentence** starts with a **capital letter**.
A **sentence** usually ends with a **full stop**.

Jimmy is not good at keeping secrets.

A Write the sentences, adding the **capital letters** and **full stops**.

1 jimmy went to school

_____

2 he was not good at keeping secrets

_____

3 libby would not tell him the secret

_____

4 he ran home to tell his Mum

_____

Spelling

or, ore, aw and au words

> Remember, these letter patterns all sound similar.

A Finish the words using **or**, **ore** or **aw**.

1 y_____n

2 sh_____t

3 h_____se

4 b_____n

5 sn_____

6 m_____

7 h_____k

8 c_____n

9 st_____

10 st_____m

11 cl_____

12 s_____

B Match the clue with the correct **au** word.

author   August   dinosaur   astronaut

1 A month of the year.   _____

2 Someone who goes to space.   _____

3 A creature that lived millions of years ago.   _____

4 Someone who writes books.   _____

Grammar

Nouns and adjectives

> **Nouns** are naming words.
> **Adjectives** are describing words.
>
> snake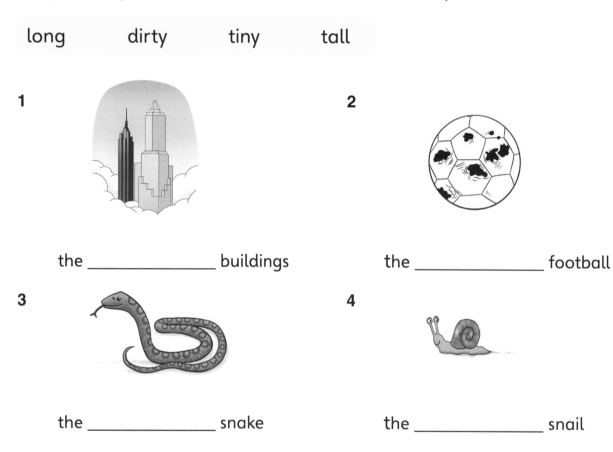
> A **little** snake

A Copy the **adjective** from the box to describe each picture.

long	dirty	tiny	tall

1

the _____ buildings

2

the _____ football

3

the _____ snake

4

the _____ snail

B Write a **describing word** and a **naming word** for each picture.

1

_____

2

_____

3

_____

4

_____

Writing

Putting events in order

Write your own simple story about something that happened to you.

1 Start by drawing a picture in each box to show the **beginning**, **middle** and **end** of your story.

2 Next to each box write a sentence describing what happens in your story. Remember to put the events in the right order.

If you can't think of your own idea here is one for you to use:
Imagine you went out for the day.
You took your favourite toy with you but it got lost.
How did you find it again?

How Do We Move?

Vocabulary

Body words

A Write the missing body part in each sentence.

knee	heart	leg	foot
back	ankle	skeleton	neck

1 My sister stood on my f_____.

2 My father has a bad b_____.

3 I can feel my h_____ beat.

4 A s_____ is made of bones.

B Write two sentences. Use a body part in each sentence.

_____

_____

Punctuation

Contractions and apostrophes

Contractions are words that have been made smaller. A letter or more than one letter is left out.

An **apostrophe** is used in place of the missing letter or letters.

I'm feeling really hungry.   I'm = I **am**

This is an **apostrophe**: '.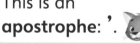

A Write the underlined words as **contractions**.

1 <u>I am</u> feeling much better.   _____

2 <u>We are</u> eating fruit.   _____

3 <u>They are</u> drinking water.   _____

4 <u>He is</u> using energy.   _____

Spelling

wa and qua words

Listen to the sound the **qua** and **wa** make.

The bucket holds a large **qua**ntity of **wa**ter.

A Read the clues. Write the answer.
Each answer is a **wa** word.

wasp   water   watch   wash   warm   swan

1 I tell the time.   _____

2 You do this to keep clean.   _____

3 You can drink me.   _____

4 I'm a bird with a long white neck. _____

5 I'm the opposite to cool.   _____

6 I'm a type of insect.   _____

B Write each of these **qua** words in a sentence.

1 squash _____

_____

2 quantity _____

_____

3 quarrel _____

_____

C How many **wa** words can you write?

_____   _____   _____

_____   _____   _____

_____   _____   _____

Grammar

Present tense verbs

> **Doing words** tell us what people, animals and things can do.
> Our heart **pumps** the blood around our body.
> Our skeleton **holds** our body in shape.

A Underline the **verb** in each sentence.

> Doing words are called **verbs.**

1 Your heart beats quickly.

2 He drinks lots of water.

3 She puts fuel in the car.

4 They work hard at school.

5 I can feel my heartbeat.

B Complete each sentence with a **present tense verb.**

1 I _____ with my ears.

2 You _____ with your eyes.

3 They _____ with their legs.

> **Present tense verbs** tell us what is happening **now**. For example: The boy **walks.** The girl **sings.**

4 He _____ with his nose.

5 We _____ with our brains.

C Use these **present tense verbs** in sentences of your own.

1 work _____

_____

2 need _____

_____

3 feels _____

_____

Writing

Using subheadings

1 Read this information about animals carefully.

Some animals are much faster than other animals. The fastest land animal is the cheetah, which lives mainly in Africa. It can run at over 100 kilometres per hour! Some animals are much bigger than other animals. The blue whale is even bigger than a basketball court. Amazingly, blue whales feed on tiny fish called krill. They can eat over 4 tonnes of krill a day.

2 What can you find out about cheetahs and blue whales?

The fastest animal

a What is the fastest land animal? _____

b Where do cheetahs live? _____

c How fast can cheetahs run? _____

The largest animal

d How big is a blue whale? _____

e What do blue whales eat? _____

f How much food do they eat each day? _____

3 Use your notes to write sentences about each animal.

a The fastest animal_____

_____

_____

b The largest animal_____

_____

_____

UNIT 3   I Wouldn't

Vocabulary

Rhyming words

A Each word from the box rhymes with another word from the box.
Write the rhyming pairs.
The first has been done to help you.

> Remember, rhyming words often have the same letter patterns.

floor	nice	house	play	cat	mice
mouse	wall	fat	hall	door	say

1 _floor_ _door_   2 _____ _____   3 _____ _____

4 _____ _____   5 _____ _____   6 _____ _____

B Write one pair of words from **Activity A** in a sentence.

_____

Punctuation

Capital letters, full stops and question marks

> A **sentence** starts with a **capital letter**.
> A **telling sentence** ends with a **full stop**.
>
>   **T**here's a mouse house in the wall**.**
>
> Some **sentences** end with a **question mark**.
> These are **asking sentences**.
>
>   **W**ill you come out to play**?**

A Put **full stops** at the end of the **telling sentences**.
Put **question marks** at the end of the **asking sentences**.

1 The mouse house has a small door_____

2 Where does the fat cat sit_____

3 The nice mice live in the mouse house_____

4 Does the cat want to play_____

5 Will the mice come out_____

Spelling

Soft c

Say these words aloud.
    cat   mice
What do you notice about the **c** sound in each word?
The **c** in mi**c**e is called a **soft c**.
It sounds more like an **s**!

A Write the **soft c** words.

1

f_____

2

j_____

3

m_____

4

r_____

5

r_____

6

i_____

B Add the **soft c** words to the table.
Sort them by looking at the letter that comes after the **soft c**.

race   icy   price
city   cinema   pencil
cereal   spicy   cycle

ci	ce	cy
_____	_____	_____
_____	_____	_____
_____	_____	_____
_____	_____	_____

C Add one more word to each column in the table.

Grammar

Making verbs using **am**, **is** and **are**

The words **am, is** and **are** help to make lots of **doing words**.

am + verb family name + ing
 I **am waiting** for the mice.

is + verb family name + ing
 The cat **is sitting** by the door.

are + verb family name + ing
 The mice **are staying** in the house.

> Doing words are called **verbs**.

A Underline the **verb** in each sentence.
 The first one has been done to help you.

> Remember these **verbs** have **two words**.

1 The cat <u>is waiting</u> for the mice.

2 The mice are hiding in their house.

3 I am visiting the city.

4 You are closing the door.

5 That cat is getting fat!

B Complete each sentence with **am, is** or **are**.

1 I _____ thinking.

2 He _____ sitting.

3 You _____ talking.

4 We _____ waiting.

5 She _____ playing.

C Use these **verbs** in sentences of your own.

1 are writing _____

 _____

2 is looking _____

 _____

3 am going _____

 _____

Writing

Rhymes

> Some poems have rhyming words.

Read these rhymes.

| In the hall | In the house |
| There's a wall. | There's a mouse. |

| Near the floor | On the mat |
| There's a door. | There's a cat. |

1   Think of your own word to complete each rhyme.
    The pictures will help you.

On the log
There's a _____

In the box
There's a _____

2   Write two more rhymes using the same rhyming pattern.

_____

_____

_____

_____

UNIT 4 How to Make a Hovering Bee

Vocabulary

Tricky words

Words with these spelling patterns can be a little tricky to learn.

| **ast** last | **ind** find | **old** gold |

A Find six words in the wordsearch.
Each word must have four letters and use one of the letter patterns.
Copy the words.

k	i	s	t	d	l	m
v	g	o	l	d	a	f
w	t	s	c	h	s	f
k	p	a	s	t	t	i
y	i	n	d	s	n	n
o	h	n	c	o	l	d
k	l	c	d	p	r	e

ast   **ind**   **old**

_____ _____ _____

_____ _____ _____

_____ _____ _____

B Add one more word to each list.

Punctuation

Capital letters and exclamation marks

All sentences begin with a **capital letter**.
Telling sentences end with a **full stop**.
Asking sentences end with a **question mark**.
Exclamations show that someone is surprised, excited or cross.

Look at this amazing bee!

A End each sentence with a **full stop** or a **question mark** or an **exclamation mark**.

1 I've spilt the paint_____

2 Fold the card in half_____

3 Where is the tissue paper_____

4 I've lost one of the eyes_____

Spelling

Words ending in **tion**

There are many words that end in **tion**.
Look at the letter patterns these words have.

sta**tion**   direc**tion**

A Copy these words and underline the **ation** or **ction** letter pattern in each.

1 location _____   2 section _____

3 selection _____   4 relation _____

5 subtraction _____   6 action _____

7 education _____   8 imagination _____

B Write each of these **tion** words in a sentence.

1 question _____

2 direction _____

3 imagination _____

4 station _____

C Can you think of three different **tion** words?

_____   _____   _____

Grammar

Conjunctions – **and, but, or**

Joining words are called **conjunctions**.

> We use the **joining word** <u>and</u> to join sentences.
> Sentence 1: Cut out shapes for the eyes.
> Sentence 2: Glue them on.
>
> Cut out shapes for the eyes **and** glue them on.
>
> You can also join sentences with **but** and **or**.
>
> Fold the card **but** don't cut it.
>
> Use white paper **or** coloured paper.

A Underline the **joining word** in each sentence.

1 I drew round the plate and cut out the circle.

2 I glued the edges but they wouldn't stick!

3 I could use white paper for the wings or I could use coloured paper.

B Join each pair of sentences using **and, but** or **or**.

1 I made a bee. It was amazing!

_____

_____

2 Do you want to make a bee? Do you want to make a butterfly?

_____

_____

C Write a **sentence** of your own about making a bee.
Use the word **but**.

_____

_____

Writing

Writing instructions

Write your own instructions for how you get to school.

> Remember, it is important to write instructions in the **correct order** or they don't make sense.
>
> If instructions are **numbered** it makes them easy to follow.
>
> They also need to be **simple** and **direct** so they can be easily understood.

Your instructions need to start from the moment you leave home and finish the moment you arrive at school.

1 _____

_____

_____

_____

_____

_____

_____

_____

_____

_____

UNIT 5 Little Red Riding Hood

Vocabulary

Opposites

A Draw a line to join each word to a word with the **opposite** meaning.

high	fat
start	huge
tiny	low
thin	weak
strong	outside
light	finish
inside	heavy

B Add **un** or **dis** to each word to make the opposite.

1 _____happy   2 _____agree   3 _____safe

4 _____approve   5 _____honest   6 _____healthy

Punctuation

Contractions of **to have**

Contractions are words that have been made smaller.
A letter or more than one letter is left out.
An **apostrophe** is used in place of the missing letter or letters.

I've got a basket.   I've = I **have**

This is an
apostrophe: '.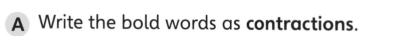

A Write the bold words as **contractions**.

1 **She has** picked red flowers.   _____

2 **They have** baked some cakes.   _____

3 **It has** grown colder.   _____

4 **I have** read the story.   _____

5 **We have** drawn a picture.   _____

Spelling

adding **ing**, **ed** and **er**

When we need to add endings to very short words there are some rules to follow.

If the letter **before** the last letter is a **vowel**, you need to **double** the last letter.

big   The trees grow bi**gger** in the wood.

If the letter **before** the last letter is **not a vowel**, you **don't need to double** the last letter.

dark cold   The wood grew dar**ker** and col**der**.

A Complete these word sums.

1 hot   + er   = _____

2 grab + ed   = _____

3 walk + ing = _____

4 mop   + ed   = _____

5 sing + er   = _____

6 run   + ing = _____

7 slip + ed   = _____

8 jump + er   = _____

Another important rule is:
If a short word ends with **e**, you need to take off the **e** before adding **ing**, **ed** or **er**.

tak**e** tak**ing**

Little Red Riding Hood is tak**ing** some flowers to her grandmother.

B Complete these word sums.

1 bounce + ing = _____

2 wave + ed   = _____

3 drive   + er   = _____

4 wipe + ed   = _____

5 write   + er   = _____

6 race   + ing = _____

7 use   + ing = _____

8 hope + ed   = _____

Grammar

Adjectives – making opposites

> **Adjectives** are describing words.   **big** and **bright** flowers
> Adjectives have **opposites**.   **small** and **pale** flowers

A Replace the **adjective** in brackets with its **opposite** from the box.

> well   wide   small   light   cloudy

1 Red Riding Hood picked some (**big**) _____ flowers.

2 Grandmother was (**ill**) _____.

3 The sky was (**sunny**) _____.

4 She went along the (**narrow**) _____ path.

5 It was (**dark**) _____ in the wood.

> You can create the **opposites** of some **adjectives** using the prefixes **un** or **dis**.
> Red Riding Hood was well. Grandmother was **un**well.
> Dark clouds appeared in the sky. The sun **dis**appeared behind the clouds.

B Add **un** or **dis** to make the **opposite** of these adjectives.

1 happy   2 like   3 honest   4 kind

_____   _____   _____   _____

C Use two of the **opposites** you have made in **Activity B** in sentences of your own.

1 _____

_____

2 _____

_____

Writing

Settings

The words that describe a **setting** build a picture in your mind of where a story is happening.

beautiful   horrible   gloomy   peaceful

dark   pleasant   sunny   frightening

1 Choose words from the box that tell you what the garden is like. Write them below.

_____

_____

_____

_____

2 Choose words from the box that tell you what the wood is like. Write them below.

_____

_____

_____

_____

3 Use one of the words about the **garden** and one of the words about the **wood** in two sentences about each setting.

   a garden setting

    1 _____

    2 _____

   b wood setting

    1 _____

    2 _____

UNIT 6 — Baby Reptiles

Vocabulary

Similar words

Remember, words which are **similar** are like each other.

A Join the similar words with a line.

say	scared	cross	ask	shut	sleepy
tired	question	close	speak	afraid	angry

B Write four of your own pairs of words.

The words must have similar meanings.

1 _____ _____   2 _____ _____

3 _____ _____   4 _____ _____

Punctuation

Capital letters, full stops and question marks

Sentences can end with a:

- full stop   Turtles cover their eggs with sand**.**
- a question mark   **W**here does the rat snake lay her eggs**?**
- an exclamation mark   **T**he baby rattle snake is breaking out of the egg**!**

A Finish each sentence with a **full stop**, a **question mark** or an **exclamation mark**.

1 Is that a lizard_____   2 That's a big snake_____

3 The turtle is digging a hole_____   4 Do crocodiles lay eggs_____

B Write a **question** about a reptile's egg.

_____

C Write an **exclamation** about a crocodile.

_____

Spelling

Unusual o words

Listen carefully to the sound the **o** makes in the word **mother**.
The **mother** rat snake lays her eggs.

A Choose words from the box to answer the clues.

loves	gloves	other	mother	brother	another
come	some	money	honey	won	done

1 I'm worn on hands when it is cold. _____

2 You need me to pay for things. _____

3 I came first in the race which means I ... _____

4 Bees make me. _____

5 I am a sister to one. _____

B Write your own word search.

Choose six unusual **o** words.

First write them in the grid below.

Then fill the spaces left with any letters.

Finally, ask someone to do your word search!

Grammar

Verbs: regular past simple tense

Past tense verbs tell us what people, animals and things **did** in the **past**.

We make the **past simple tense** like this:

Verb family name + **ed**   cover + ed = **covered**

Verb family name ending in e + **d**   provide + d = **provided**

If the verb family name ends in **e**, just add **d**.

A Underline the **past simple verb** in each sentence.

1 We <u>learned</u> about baby reptiles.

2 They stayed away from the turtle's nest.

3 I painted a picture of a reptile egg.

4 The baby rat-snake hatched today.

5 "That's a baby rat-snake!" she shouted.

B Do the word sums to make the **past simple tense**.

1 to smile   +   d   _____smiled_____

The first one is done for you.

2 to laugh   +   ed   _____

3 to joke   +   d   _____

C Use these **past simple verbs** in sentences of your own.

1 breathed _____

_____

2 watched _____

_____

3 covered _____

_____

Flow diagrams

We can put information into a flow diagram that shows the order in which things happen.

Choose something to draw and write about in this flow diagram.

It can be something you do (like brushing your teeth) or something you know about (like planting a seed).

My flow diagram shows the three stages of _____

_____

Stage 1

Stage 2

Stage 3

UNIT 7 A Book Cover

Vocabulary

Transport words

Use a different word in each sentence.

A Write the different transport words in the sentences.

| train | bike | car | plane | boat | lorry |

1 My father flew on a _____ to Sri Lanka.

2 We took a _____ up the Indus River.

3 The _____ carried the bananas to market.

4 My mother drove her _____ to the shop.

5 The _____ arrived at the crowded station.

6 I rode my _____ to school.

Punctuation

Commas in lists

When we write a **list** in a sentence we use **commas**.
We can join the last two things in the list with **and**.

Mr Timms is carrying a briefcase, an umbrella **and** a newspaper.

A Add the missing **commas**.

1 I travel by bike bus and train.

2 The station was hot crowded and noisy.

3 I ride my bike to school to the shops and to the library.

4 Buses bikes and cars have wheels.

5 Kim Green wrote about a train a car and a holiday.

Spelling

y and ey endings

> Listen to the sound the **y** makes at the end of each word in bold.
>
> *Mr Timms Learns to* **Fly**   A **funny** book
>
> Sometimes the **y** at the end of a word sounds like **i** in **b̲i̲ke**.
>
> Sometimes the **y** at the end of a word sounds like **ee** in **b̲ee̲**.

A Write four words that end in **y** and sounds like **i**.

_____   _____

_____   _____

B Write four words that end in **y** and sounds like **ee**.

_____   _____

_____   _____

> When adding **s** to words that end in **y** remember these rules:
>
> If the letter **before** the **y** is a vowel just add **s**.
>
>   monk̲e̲y + **s** = monkey**s**
>
> If the letter **before** the **y** is any other letter **drop the y** and **add ies**.
>
>   butterfly + **s** = butterfl**ies**

> We add **s** to nouns to show there is more than one:
> **one** monkey   **two** monkey**s**
> **one** butterfly   **two** butterfl**ies**

C Add **s** to each of these words ending in **y**.

1 monkey _____   2 fly   _____

3 reply   _____   4 valley _____

5 jelly   _____   6 story _____

7 chimney _____   8 key   _____

Grammar

Compound nouns

> There are many different types of **nouns**.
>
> **Common nouns** are the names of ordinary things.
>   **book**
>
> **Proper nouns** are special naming words for people, places, days and months.
> **Mr Timms**
>
> **Compound nouns** are made by joining two nouns together.
>   news + paper   **newspaper**

A Write the **compound nouns** for each of these.

1

_____

2

_____

3

_____

4

_____

5

_____

6

_____

B Use a dictionary to find two **compound nouns** for each word.

1 hill   a _____   b _____

2 water   a _____   b _____

3 tea   a _____   b _____

C Use one of the **compound nouns** you have written in **Activity B** in a sentence of your own.

_____

_____

A book cover

Use this template to help you plan a front cover and back cover for a storybook.

Front cover

Title:_____

Illustration:_____

Author:_____

Back cover

Information about the story:_____

_____

_____

_____

_____

What people who liked the book said about it:_____

_____

_____

_____

Titles of other books by the same author:_____

_____

_____

_____

Published by: _____

_____

Bridges

Vocabulary

Words within words

A How many small words does the word **sometimes** have?

Write the words.

_____   _____   _____

_____   _____   _____

> You can use a dictionary to help!

B Challenge! Can you find two words that contain:

1 One smaller word   _____   _____

2 Two smaller words   _____   _____

3 Three smaller words   _____   _____

4 More than three smaller words   _____   _____

Punctuation

Contractions with **not**

> **Contractions** are words that have been made smaller.
> A letter or more than one letter is left out.
> An **apostrophe** is used in place of the missing letter or letters.
>
> Bridges must be strong so they **don't** fall down.
>
> don't = do not

> This is an **apostrophe**: '.

A Write the bold words as **contractions**.

1 I **cannot** find the index in this book.   _____

2 Modern beam bridges **are not** made of wood.   _____

3 That bridge **is not** safe!   _____

4 Beam bridges **do not** hang from cables.   _____

5 This book **has not** got an index.   _____

Spelling

soft g

> Say these words aloud:
>   long   bridge
>
> What do you notice about the **g** sound in each word?
>
> The **g** in bri**dg**e is called a **soft g**.
> It sounds more like a **j**!

A Circle the words with a **soft g**.

ledge	goat	smudge
tangle	badge	stage
sing	package	page
garage	urgent	tragic
garden	single	bridge
giraffe	tiger	eagle

B Which word has a **soft g** <u>and</u> a **hard g** in **Activity A**?

_____

C Write two funny sentences.
   Each sentence must include three **soft g** words.

1 _____

   _____

   _____

2 _____

   _____

Grammar

Adjectives: comparatives with er

Adjectives are describing words.
They tell us more about people, animals, places and things.

   a **long** bridge

Adjectives can describe the **difference** between **two things**.

   a **long** bridge
long + **er** = a **long<u>er</u>** bridge

Longer is a **comparative adjective**.

A Underline the **comparative adjective** in each sentence.

1 My pencil is sharper than yours.

2 You can run faster than me.

3 This stone is smaller than that one.

4 That river is deeper than this one.

5 This cable is thicker than that one.

B Add **er** to the adjective in brackets to make a **comparative adjective**.

1 My brother is _____ than yours   (old)

2 This pillow is _____ than that one.   (soft)

3 That bridge is _____ than this one.   (strong)

4 I can shout _____ than you.   (loud)

5 That tower is _____ than this one.   (tall)

C Use these **comparative adjectives** in sentences of your own.

1 warmer   _____

    _____

    _____

2 fresher   _____

    _____

    _____

Writing

Writing an index

Use the information on this page to help you create an index.
Here are the names of some bridges with page numbers.
The names have to be put in alphabetical order to make an index.

Waterloo Bridge – p32   Zambezi Bridge – p35   Narmada River Bridge – p31

Akashi Kaikyō Bridge – p5   Humber Bridge – p19   Dabong Bridge – p10

Tower Bridge – p29   Bridge of Sighs – p7   Golden Gate Bridge – p13

Sydney Harbour Bridge – p24   Lansdowne Bridge – p22   JK Bridge – p40

1   Write the names of each bridge next to the letter it begins with.

A   <u>Akashi–Kaikyō Bridge</u>   N   _____

B   _____   O   _____

C   _____   P   _____

D   _____   Q   _____

E   _____   R   _____

F   _____   S   _____

G   _____   T   _____

H   _____   U   _____

I   _____   V   _____

J   _____   W   _____

K   _____   X   _____

L   _____   Y   _____

M   _____   Z   _____

2   Copy out your alphabetical list and add the correct page numbers
     to make an index.

Lara's Letter

Vocabulary

Activity words

A Add the words in the word box to the sentences.

| reading | swimming | singing | riding |

1 I love _____ in the sea.

2 I enjoy _____ books.

3 I like _____ songs I know.

4 I love _____ my bike to school.

B List three more activities.

_____   _____   _____

C Use one of the words from **Activity B** in a sentence of your own.

_____

_____

Punctuation

Possessive nouns

Possessive nouns tell you who **owns** something.
They have an **apostrophe** and an **s** at the end.

Lara**'s** letter = the letter belonging to Lara

Aimee**'s** hand = the hand belonging to Aimee

This is an
apostrophe: '.

A Write each of these in a shorter way using a **possessive noun**.

1 the bat belonging to Dad   _____

2 the camera belonging to Mum   _____

3 the snorkel belonging to Aimee   _____

4 the holiday belonging to Lara   _____

Spelling

y + er, y + est, y + ed

> When **er**, **est** or **ed** is added to words that end with **y** we usually change the **y** to an **i**.
>
> smell**y** + er = smell**i**er
>
> smell**y** + est = smell**i**est

> They were fed the smelliest food I've ever smelt!

A Finish this table, adding **er** and **est** to the words ending in **y**.

> We don't change **y** to an **i** if the letter before the **y** is a vowel!

	+ er	+ est
happy	happier	
muddy		muddiest
funny		
grumpy		
lazy		

B Choose three of the words from the table and write them in sentences.

1 _____

2 _____

3 _____

C Add **ed** to each of these words.

1 cry _____   2 dry _____   3 try _____

Grammar

Past progressive tense

> The words **was** and **were** help to make lots of **verbs**.
>
>   **was** + verb family name + ing   I **was snorkelling** in the sea.
>   **were** + verb family name + ing   We **were playing** cricket.
>
> These verbs are called the **past progressive tense**.

A Underline the **past progressive tense verbs** in each sentence.
The first has been done for you.

Was is **singular**.
Were is **plural**.

1 I <u>was writing</u> a letter home.

2 We were watching the crocodiles at the wildlife centre.

3 They were going for a walk.

B These sentences are in the **present progressive tense**.
Change each underlined verb to the **past progressive tense**.

1 Lara <u>is writing</u> to her Mum and Dad.

   _____ _____

2 They <u>are doing</u> so many things.

   _____ _____

3 They <u>are swimming</u> at the Beach Park.

   _____ _____

4 Aimee <u>is taking</u> pictures of the crocodiles.

   _____ _____

C Complete each sentence with a **past progressive verb**.

1 Ben and Aimee _____

   _____ in the sea.

2 Uncle Harry _____

   _____ the wildlife centre.

3 Lara's Mum _____

   _____ the letter.

Writing

Writing a letter

Use this page to write a letter.

Look carefully at how your letter needs to be laid out.

Think about **who** you will write it to and **what** you will write about, then lay it out below.

Your address

_____

_____

_____

_____

The date today

_____

Who the letter is to

Dear _____ ,

_____

_____

_____

_____

_____

_____

_____

_____

from _____

Vocabulary

Word families

> Remember, some words can be a part of a **family** of words.

A Write a word in the same family as each of these.

1 visit _____visitor_____

2 build _____

3 interest _____

4 tour _____

5 safe _____

6 enjoy _____

7 list _____

8 count _____

9 play _____

10 open _____

B Write as many different words as you can that all belong to this family word.

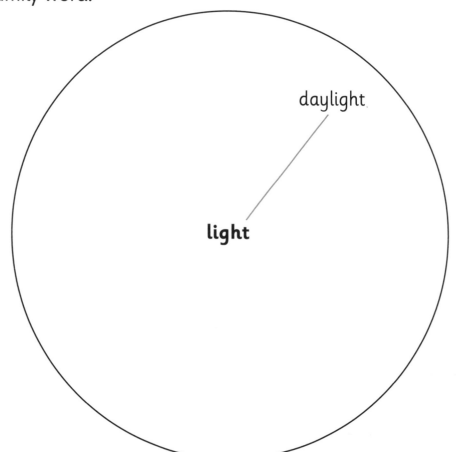

daylight

light

Punctuation

Speech marks

> We use **speech marks** (" ") when we write the actual words someone **says**.
>
>   "We've got a puncture!" said Dad.

A Add the missing **speech marks**.

Look for the **spoken words**.

1   We've got a puncture! said Dad.

2   Where is the spare tyre? asked Mum.

3   It's in the boot! said Dad.

4   All the cases are in the boot, said Mum.

5   I know! said Dad.

Spelling

Silent letters

> Some words have **silent letters** that we don't hear when we say the words aloud.
>
>   **w**rong has a silent **w**

A Circle the words that have a **silent letter w**.

wrinkle   swan   watch   swim   wrist   wrong

write   water   wrap   answer   whole   window

B Circle the **silent letter** in each of these words.

1 knot   2 wrap   3 knee

Watch out! Not all silent letters are at the beginning of the word.

4 sign   5 know   6 writer

C Each of these words has a silent **k** or silent **w** missing. Rewrite the words correctly.

1 nock _____   2 rist _____

3 reck _____   4 nee _____

Grammar

Making a verb into a noun

Nouns are the name of things. **wheel car**
We can make **nouns** from verbs by adding **r** or **er**.

verb	noun
to **farm**	farm**er**

A Match the **nouns** in the box with the correct picture.

reader	gardener	climber

1   2   3

_____   _____   _____

B Make these verbs into **nouns**.

1 to jump _____   2 to write _____

3 to bake _____   4 to walk _____

5 to drum _____   6 to skate _____

C Use two of the **nouns** you have made in **Activity B** in sentences of
your own.

1 _____

_____

2 _____

_____

Writing

Fiction and non-fiction

Colour the picture of the bicycle neatly and read the labels.

Non-fiction texts contain true facts. They provide us with information.

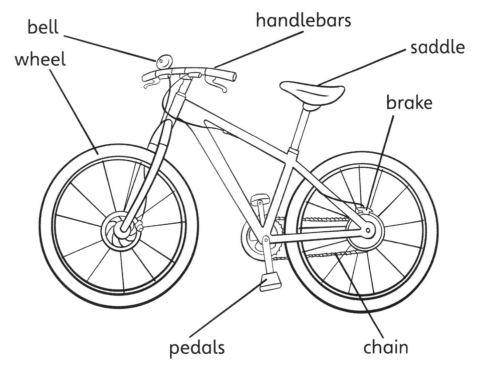

bell

wheel

handlebars

saddle

brake

pedals

chain

1 Write a description of the bicycle.
  Write about what colour it is.
  Write about the parts it has.

_____

_____

_____

_____

_____

2 Think of something that could happen
  to the bike in a story.
  Write down your idea.

Fiction books have been made up. They include stories.

_____

_____

_____

The Three Billy Goats Gruff

Vocabulary

Sound words

A Finish these sentences with an animal sound.

squawk	miaow	hiss	heehaw

1 The snake goes _____.

2 The donkey goes _____.

3 The cat goes _____.

4 The crow goes _____.

B Write a sound that each of these animals makes.

1 a sheep _____   2 a duck _____

3 a bee _____   4 a chicken _____

5 a lion _____   6 a mouse _____

Punctuation

Possessive nouns

> **Possessive nouns** tell you who **owns** something.
> They have an **apostrophe** and an **s** at the end.
> the bridge belonging to the troll = the **troll's** bridge

This is an **apostrophe**: '.

A Write each of these in a shorter way using a **possessive noun**.

1 the beak belonging to the chicken _____

2 the cub belonging to the lion _____

3 the tree belonging to the farmer _____

4 the cat belonging to the boy _____

5 the hole belonging to the mouse _____

Spelling

al and all words

A Match each word to the correct picture.

wall   waterfall   ball   sandal   pedal   tall

1

_____

2

_____

3

_____

4

_____

5

_____

6

_____

Remember, when we use the **all** sound at the beginning of a word we drop one **l**.

B Mark this spelling test.
Tick the words spelt correctly.
Rewrite the words spelt incorrectly.

1 already ⬭ _____

2 capitall ⬭ _____

3 bal ⬭ _____

4 allso ⬭ _____

5 tall ⬭ _____

6 hospital ⬭ _____

7 allmost ⬭ _____

8 always ⬭ _____

Grammar

Adverbs with ly

Adverbs tell us more about **how** something is done.

The troll roars. The troll roars **loudly**.

How does the troll roar?　　**loudly**

 An **adverb adds** to a **verb**.

A Underline the **adverb** in each sentence.

1 The goat ate greedily.

2 The farmer ran quickly.

3 The lion roared loudly.

4 The cat miaowed softly.

5 The wind blew strongly.

B Complete the sentences with **adverbs** from the box.

| brightly | quickly | quietly | loudly |

1 The boy whispered _____ to his friend.

2 The grass grew _____ after the rain.

3 The people shouted _____ at the football game.

4 The sun shone _____ in the sky.

C Complete these sentences with **adverbs** of your own.

1 The hen clucked _____.

2 The mouse squeaked _____.

3 The horse galloped _____.

Describing characters

Use this page to make a poster about a character from a story.

1 Choose a character.
2 Make a poster about the character you have chosen.
   a Write the name of the character as the title.
   b Draw a picture of the character.
   c Write some sentences to describe what the character looks like.
   d Write a sentence about the character's personality.

Vocabulary

Linking words

The Chatterbox Turtle

1 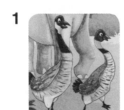 2  3  4  5

A With the help of the strip above, write a summary of the story. Use these linking words.

First _____

Next _____

Then _____

Soon _____

Finally _____

B Read your sentences aloud. Do they make sense?

Punctuation

Contractions

Remember, **contractions** are words that have been made smaller. An **apostrophe** is used in place of a missing letter or letters.

We are   **We're**

This is an **apostrophe**: '.

A Write these words **without** the **apostrophe**.

1 don't _____   2 won't _____   3 he's _____

4 we've _____   5 they're _____   6 I'm _____

B Write these words **with** an **apostrophe**.

1 she has _____   2 it is _____   3 must not _____

4 you have _____   5 you are _____   6 did not _____

Spelling

un and dis prefixes

When we add the prefixes **un** and **dis** to the beginning
of a word, the new word has the **opposite** meaning.
  All the animals **dis**agreed with Turtle.
  They thought he was **un**able to stop talking!

A Finish these sentences with a word from the word box.

disobeyed   disliked   unsure   untie   unhappy

1 Turtle _____ his muddy pool and wanted to go
   somewhere better.

2 At first Turtle was _____ about flying.

3 Turtle _____ the geese when they told him not to talk.

4 Turtle was _____ when the other animals laughed at him.

B Write two sentences: one before the prefix
is added and one after the prefix is added.

> Notice how the
> meaning changes when
> the **prefix** is added.

1 fold _____

_____

2 unfold _____

_____

3 agree _____

_____

4 disagree _____

_____

5 cover _____

_____

6 uncover _____

_____

Grammar

Using adjectives to compare

Adjectives are describing words. They tell us more about people, animals, places and things.

   a **long** stick

Adjectives can describe the **difference** between **two things**.

   a **long** stick   long + **er** = a **long<u>er</u>** stick

Adjectives can describe the **difference** between **three or more things**.

   a **long** stick   long + **est** = the **long<u>est</u>** stick

> **Longer** is a **comparative adjective**. **Longest** is a **superlative adjective**.

A Underline the **superlative adjective** in each sentence.

1 Turtle is the biggest chatterbox of all the animals.

2 The geese are the kindest birds.

3 This is the shortest stick.

B Add **est** to the adjective in brackets to make a **superlative adjective**.

1 Turtle is the _____ he has ever been. (quiet)

2 This the _____ I have ever flown. (high)

C Write the **adjectives** from the box under the correct heading.

| freshest | warmer | fresh | cold | fresher |
| warm | coldest | warmest | colder | |

adjective	comparative adjective	superlative adjective

Writing

Writing a description

A **description** of a setting or character helps the reader to picture the story in their mind.

Our **senses** can help us to write good descriptions.
Our senses are what we **touch**, **taste**, **smell**, **feel** and **see**.

1   Look again at this picture of the muddy pool the Turtle lives in.

2   Write a description of this setting.
    Write about the things you can see, touch, taste, hear and smell.

_____

_____

_____

_____

_____

_____

_____

_____

_____

A Woodland Dictionary

Vocabulary

Compound words

> Remember, a **compound word** is when two words are put together to make a new word.

A Write a word from the box in front of each word below, to make a compound word.

bath	farm	play	skate
foot	wood	sun	tooth

1 _____ brush   2 _____ shine

3 _____ board   4 _____ ground

5 _____ land   6 _____ room

7 _____ house   8 _____ print

B Write three more compound words.

_____   _____   _____

Punctuation

Commas in lists

> When we write a **list** in a sentence we use **commas** between the items in the list. We can join the last two things in the list with **and, but** and **or**.
>
> The tree has bark, branches **and** a trunk.
>
> That tree has bark, a trunk, branches **but** no leaves.
>
> Are you drawing branches, the trunk **or** the leaves?

A Add the missing **commas**. Add the missing **conjunctions**.

1 These leaves are large green _____ flat.

2 Forests grow in Europe Asia _____ not Antarctica.

3 Is this leaf from an oak an elm _____ a neem?

4 We have learned about trees shrubs _____ forests.

Spelling

ar words

A Finish the word sums.

1 ar + m = _____

2 st + ar = _____

3 d + ar + k = _____

4 b + ar + k = _____

5 st + ar + t = _____

6 sm + ar + t = _____

B Sort the words into the table of letter patterns.
Then add another word in each gap in the table.

start   star   mark   jar
shark   yard   dart   hard

ar words	art words	ard words	ark words

C Circle the words where the **ar** makes an **or** sound.

sharp   forward   warm

     ward   scarf   start

towards   marsh

53

Grammar

Subordinating conjunctions: **so** and **because**

> **Conjunctions** are joining words.

We use the **conjunctions** to join sentences.

The tree has large branches **and** it has thin leaves.

The tree has large branches **but** it has no leaves.

This tree could be deciduous **or** it could be coniferous.

Evergreens don't lose their leaves **so** they are always green.

Evergreens are always green **because** they don't lose their leaves.

A Underline the **conjunction** in each sentence.

1 I went to the forest because I wanted some cones.

2 They planted more trees so the woodland would be bigger.

3 I have planted shrubs in the garden but I have not planted trees.

B Join each pair of sentences with **so** or **because**.

> Remember, you only need **one capital letter** and **one full stop**.

1 The tree has been cut down. It was struck by lightning.

_____

_____

2 The tree was struck by lightning. It has been cut down.

_____

_____

C Write **two sentences** about a tree.
Join them with **so** or **because**.

Sentence I: _____

_____

Sentence 2: _____

_____

Joined sentence: _____

_____

Writing

Dictionary definitions

Dictionaries help us to spell words.
They also explain the meaning of each word.
This explanation is called a **definition**.
The words in dictionaries are arranged in **alphabetical order**.

Write your own dictionary of topic words.

1   Choose a topic you are interested in.
    Write five words linked to the topic. Each word must begin with
    a different letter.

2   Now write each word in alphabetical order with a short definition.

_____   _____

                    _____

_____   _____

                    _____

_____   _____

                    _____

_____   _____

                    _____

_____   _____

                    _____

UNIT 14 A Dragon in the Classroom

Vocabulary

Remember, words which are **similar** are like each other.

Similar words

A Circle all the words which are similar to the word **talk**.

speak	step	say	jump	answer	tell	sleep
crouch	reply	clap	dig	eat	chat	gossip

B Copy the similar word hidden in the letters. Write the word.

1 walk   pstrollhyrs   **2 repair**   lkrdefixsa   **3 offer**   mugivedsad

_____ _____ _____

Punctuation

Punctuation round-up

These are the **punctuation** marks that have been covered so far.

full stop: comes at the end of a telling sentence   .

question mark: comes at the end of an asking sentence   ?

exclamation mark: comes at the end of a sentence that shows someone is shouting, surprised or cross   !

comma: separates items in a list   ,

apostrophe: shows where a letter or letters have been left out or shows who owns something   ,

speech marks: shows which words are spoken   " "

A Add the missing **punctuation marks**.

1 Have you seen the dragon

2 That s a fierce dragon

3 The dragon is made of clocks cardboard and a waste-bin

4 The dragon s tongue is an old tie, he said

Spelling

Using suffixes

> Sometimes, a group of letters is added to the end of a word. This is called a **suffix**. Here are some suffixes: **ly**, **ful**, **less**, **ness** and **ment**.
>
> If **y** on the end of a word sounds like **ee** as in **bee**, when you add a suffix you need to change the **y** to an **i** and then add the suffix.
>
> silly + ness = silliness

A Add the missing suffixes **ful**, **ly**, **less**, **ness** and **ment** to each of these words. The pictures will help.

1

care_____

2

bright_____

3

quick_____

4

agree_____

5

dark_____

6

pay_____

B Add a suffix to each of these words.

1 silly _____   2 lazy _____   3 happy _____

C Write each of the words you have made in **Activity B** into a sentence.

1 _____

_____

2 _____

_____

3 _____

_____

Grammar

Adverbs for **when** and **where**

Some adverbs tell us **how** something is done.
  The teacher laughed **happily**.
Some adverbs tell us **when** something is done.
  I saw the dragon **today**.
Some adverbs tell us **where** something is done.
  I have put the dragon **outside**.

An **adverb adds** to a **verb**.

A Write the **adverbs** from the box under the correct heading.

yesterday	neatly	inside	later	heavily	upstairs
often	early	quietly	there	everywhere	wisely

adverb – how	adverb – where	adverb – when

B Use these **adverbs** in sentences of your own.

1 sweetly _____

_____

2 usually _____

_____

3 somewhere _____

_____

Writing

Dragon poem

Write your own dragon poem.

1   First draw the dragon you are going to write about.

2   Now finish these lines to make your own poem.

There's a dragon in the classroom:

its body is _____,

its head is _____,

its eyes are _____,

its legs are _____,

its claws are _____,

its tongue is _____,

I would like to name it _____.

UNIT 15 Christopher's Bicycle

Vocabulary

Homophones

A Underline the homophones in these sentences.

1 I knew it was time for a new bag when my old one broke.

2 My sister and I ate eight cakes.

3 I can see the sea from my bedroom window.

> Remember, **homophones** are words that sound the same but are spelt differently and have different meanings.

B Write a sentence for each of these homophones.

1 saw _____

  sore _____

2 right _____

  write _____

Punctuation

Punctuation round-up

> These are the **punctuation marks** that have been covered so far.
>
> **full stop:** .   **question mark:** ?
>
> **exclamation mark:** !   **comma:** ,
>
> **apostrophe:** '   **speech marks:** " "

A **Punctuate** the passage.

Mr Nibble s shed was where he made things Mr Nibble was working on something TOP SECRET Christopher could hear banging sawing and drilling

What are you making asked Christopher

It s a surprise shouted Mr Nibble

60

Spelling

Word endings: **le**, **el**, **al** and **il**

sta**le**		pen**cil**
		la**bel**
		ped**al**

A Match the correct word from the word box to each picture.

pedal	handle	medal	rectangle
paddle	model	nostril	signal
pencil	camel	fossil	tunnel

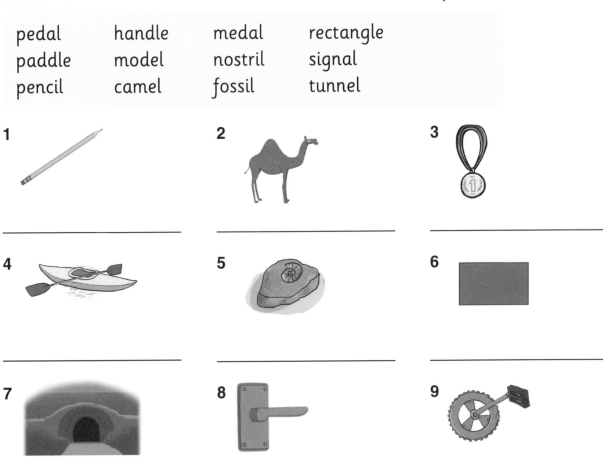

1 _____

2 _____

3 _____

4 _____

5 _____

6 _____

7 _____

8 _____

9 _____

B Write a rhyming word, using the same word ending, for each of these words.

1 jangle ____tangle____   2 candle _____

3 gravel _____   4 vowel _____

5 metal _____   6 rumble _____

Grammar

Comparative and superlative adverbs with **er** and **est**

> **Adverbs** can describe the difference between **two actions**. These are called **comparative adverbs**.
>
> Posie worked **hard**.   Poppy worked **harder**.
>
> **Adverbs** can describe the difference between **three or more actions**. These are called **superlative adverbs**.
>
> Posie worked **hard**.   Poppy worked **hard<u>er</u>**.
>
> Christopher worked the **hard<u>est</u>**.

A Write the **adverbs** from the box under the correct heading.

> fast   hardest   later   near   faster   nearer
> fastest   late   nearest   hard   harder   latest

adverb	comparative adverb	superlative adverb

B Use these **adverbs** in sentences of your own.

1 later _____

_____

2 nearest _____

_____

3 hard _____

_____

Writing

Writing stories

Stories need a **beginning, middle** and **end**.
At the **beginning** of the story *Christopher's Bicycle* Christopher was given a recycled bicycle.
This gave him an idea.
In the **middle** of the story Christopher collected things that were going to be thrown away, and he recycled them to make newspaper bags, bird feeders and colourful vases. He then rode back to town on his bicycle with the recycled items.

What happens next?
Finish the story in your own words.
Here is the first sentence:

They loaded Christopher's bicycle with recycled goodies and Christopher set off for the town.

_____

_____

_____

_____

_____

_____

_____

BOOK 1

Word Practice

Number words

Trace and write the number words.

Colour the numbers.

10 ten   ten   _____ _____

20 twenty   twenty   _____ _____

30 thirty   thirty   _____ _____

40 forty   forty   _____ _____

50 fifty   fifty   _____ _____

60 sixty   sixty   _____ _____

70 seventy   seventy   _____ _____

80 eighty   eighty   _____ _____

90 ninety   ninety   _____ _____

Describing words

Trace and write the describing words.
Colour the pictures.

Describing words are called **adjectives**.

 fast   fast _____ _____

 slow   slow _____ _____

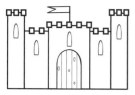 old   old _____ _____

 new   new _____ _____

 big   big _____ _____

 small   small _____ _____

 happy   happy _____ _____

 sad   sad _____ _____

Naming words

Trace and write the naming words.
Colour the pictures.

Naming words are called **nouns**.

 baby   baby _____ _____

 bag   bag _____ _____

 bee   bee _____ _____

 bridge   bridge _____ _____

 bus   bus _____ _____

 city   city _____ _____

 flower   flower _____ _____

 monkey   monkey _____ _____

 shoes shoes _____ _____

 pencil pencil _____ _____

 plane plane _____ _____

 scissors scissors _____ _____

 shop shop _____ _____

 storm storm _____ _____

 train train _____ _____

 water water _____ _____

67

Doing words

Trace and write the doing words.

Doing words are called **verbs**.

   climb   climb   _____   _____

   cut   cut   _____   _____

   cycle   cycle   _____   _____

   dislike   dislike   _____   _____

   drink   drink   _____   _____

   drive   drive   _____   _____

   fly   fly   _____   _____

   make   make   _____   _____

 sing   sing _____ _____

 swim   swim _____ _____

 talk   talk _____ _____

 think   think _____ _____

 throw   throw _____ _____

 wash   wash _____ _____

 watch   watch _____ _____

 write   write _____ _____

Joining words

Trace and write the joining words.

Joining words are called **conjunctions**.

and   and   and   _____   _____

or   or   or   _____   _____

but   but   but   _____   _____

so   so   so   _____   _____

because   because   because   _____   _____

Add a joining word to each sentence.

I like to eat bananas _____ apples.

I will read a story _____ I will play a game.

I like running and swimming _____ not dancing.

I will go to the library _____ I can find a book.

I will drink some water _____ I am thirsty.

Months of the year

Trace and write the months of the year.
Remember to use a capital letter.

Months of the year are **proper nouns**.

January   January   _____   _____

February   February   _____   _____

March   March   _____   _____

April   April   _____   _____

May   May   _____   _____

June   June   _____   _____

July   July   _____   _____

August   August   _____   _____

September   September   _____   _____

October   October   _____   _____

November   November   _____   _____

December   December   _____   _____

BOOK 2 Glossary

adjective (describing word) a word that tells us more about someone or something – for example: *loud*

adverb a word that tells us more about how something is done – for example: *loudly*

apostrophe a punctuation mark (') that is used to show that a letter or letters have been missed out (*didn't*); or that the noun is the owner of another noun (*the boy's bag*)

comma a punctuation mark (,) that is used to show a pause in a sentence; commas are also used to separate words in a list

comparative adjective a word that describes the difference between two things – for example: *longer*

comparative adverb an adverb that describes the difference between two actions – for example: *louder*

compound word a word that is made by joining two words together – for example: *football*

conjunction (joining word) a word used to join two sentences – for example: *and*

contraction when a letter or letters are left out of a word, and replaced with an apostrophe – for example: *we're*

fiction when a book or piece of writing has been made up, including stories, poems and plays

homophone words that sound the same, but are spelt differently and have a different meaning – for example: *son* and *sun*

index a list of the topics in a book, found at the end of the book

non-fiction when a book or piece of writing contains true information or facts

opposite a word that describes something that is the most different from something else – for example: *hot/cold*; *up/down*

possessive noun a noun that tells you who owns something using an apostrophe – for example: *Indre's book*

prefix a group of letters that is added to the beginning of a word and changes its meaning – for example: *dis*, *mis*, *re*, *un*

speech marks a pair of punctuation marks ("") placed around the spoken words when writing direct speech

suffix a word ending

superlative adverb an adverb that describes the difference between three or more actions – for example: *loudest*

word family a group of words that have the same root word – for example: *help*, *helpful* and *helper* are all part of the same word family